Table of Contents

Introduction 1

Baked Mahi-Mahi with Dill Sauce 2

Baked Possum 3

Baked Walleye with Carrots 4

Bass with Avocado Sauce 5

Blackened Salmon 6

Bombay Monkfish 7

Brandied Orange Rabbit With Mushrooms 8

Cajun Crappie 9

Cajun Frog Legs 10

California Wild Duck Stew 11

Carolina Roast Venison 12

Carp with Red Sauce 13

Catfish with Parsley-Pecan Sauce 14

Chinese Venison 15

Cream Of Crab Soup 16

Crab Stuffing 17

Crawdad Gumbo 18

Deviled Rabbit 19

Duck in Guinness and Honey 20

Duck and Roasted Walnut Salad 21

Fricassee of Rabbit 22

Fried Rocky Mountain Oysters 23

Roast Goose with Wild Rice 24

Table of Contents

- Italian Roast Pheasant ... 25
- Lemon-Coriander Game Hens ... 26
- Medieval Sweet and Sour Fish ... 27
- Ostrich and Shrimp in Roasted Garlic Sauce ... 28
- Oriental Glazed Duck ... 29
- Chunky Oyster Chowder ... 30
- Panfish Creole ... 31
- Partridge Casserole ... 32
- Pheasant Jubilee ... 33
- Pheasant in Spiced Sour Cream ... 34
- Rabbit In Tarragon Sauce ... 35
- Rack of Venison With Mushrooms ... 36
- Roast Duck with Port-Garlic Sauce ... 37
- Roast Goose with Baked Apples ... 39
- Roast Quail Stuffed with Foie Gras ... 40
- Roast Wild Turkey ... 41
- Salmon Pate ... 42
- Scotched Pheasant ... 43
- Baked Seafood Au Gratin ... 44
- Spicy Blackened Catfish ... 45
- Tarragon Trout ... 46
- Trout with Red Onion and Orange Relish ... 47
- Venison Bigos ... 48
- Venison Cutlets with Apples ... 49

Table of Contents

Venison Sirloin 50

Venison Stew 51

Venison Roast Marinated in Buttermilk 53

Wild Goose Chase 54

Baked Mahi-Mahi with Dill Sauce

1/4 cup sour cream
1/4 cup plain yogurt
1 tablespoon mayonnaise or salad dressing
1 tablespoon minced fresh dill or 1 teaspoon dried dill
1/2 teaspoon Dijon mustard
1/8 teaspoon bottled hot pepper sauce
Salt & pepper to taste
2 Mahi-Mahi Steaks
1 tablespoon vegetable oil
1 tablespoon lemon juice
Salt
White pepper

Combine our sour cream, yogurt, mayonnaise, mustard, and hot sauce. Stir in dill; add salt and pepper to taste. Blend well. Allow to stand at least 1/2 hour to blend flavors. Serve at room temperature. May be refrigerated up to 24 hours.
Pat fish dry with paper towels. Combine oil and lemon juice; brush on both sides of fish. Season lightly with salt and white pepper. Place an inch apart in a lightly oiled baking dish. Bake at 450F for approximately 15 mintues. When fish tests are done, transfer to warm plates. Spoon Dill Sauce over fish.

Baked Possum

1 large possum, skinned, dressed, and washed
1 quart beer
4 tablespoons Tabasco sauce
1 1/2 tablespoons salt
2 onions, chopped
1 clove garlic, minced
2 tablespoons Worcestershire sauce
4 sweet potatoes
2 ribs celery, chopped
1 oz. whiskey

Mix the beer, whiskey, salt, Tabasco sauce, and Worcestershire sauce together. Place possum in a large roasting pan. Sprinkle the celery, onions, and the garlic all over the possum. Pour the liquid mixture over the possum as well. Cover and refrigerate overnight.

Preheat oven to 350F. Place the sweet potatoes around the possum. Bake covered for 1 1/2 hours. Baste once or twice with the marinade from the pan as the possum cooks.

Baked Walleye with Carrots

1 1/2 pounds walleye fillets, skin removed
2 cups grated carrots
3 tablespoons margarine or butter, melted
2 tablespoons lemon juice
1/4 teaspoon ground thyme
Salt to taste
3 tablespoons margarine or butter
3 1/2 tablespoons flour
Salt and pepper to taste
1/3 cup milk

Heat oven to 450F. Spray a 13 x 9-inch baking dish with nonstick vegetable cooking spray. Arrange fillets, slightly overlapping, in prepared dish. Set aside. In medium bowl, combine carrots, melted margarine, juice, thyme and salt. Spread mixture evenly over fillets. Cover with foil. Bake for 25 to 30 minutes, or until fish is firm and opaque and just begins to flake. Drain liquid from fish into a 2-cup measure. Cover fish with foil to keep warm. Set aside. Add water to liquid in cup to equal 1 1/3 cups.

In a 1-quart saucepan, melt 3 tablespoons margarine over medium heat. Stir in flour, salt and pepper. Blend in cooking liquid mixture and milk. Cook for 5 to 7 minutes or until mixture thickens and bubbles, stirring constantly. Pour sauce evenly over fish and serve over hot rice or linguine.

Bass with Avocado Sauce

1 small ripe avocado coarsely chopped
1/4 cup skim milk
1 tablespoon lime juice
1 garlic clove minced
1 dash hot sauce
2 tablespoons lemon juice
1 tablespoon soy sauce
1 teaspoon lemon rind grated
1 teaspoon Dijon mustard
16 ounces bass fillets
1/3 cup dry bread crumbs fine
 vegetable cooking spray

Combine the first 5 ingredients in a blender; cover and process until smooth. Set mixture aside. Combine lemon juice and next 3 ingredients in a shallow dish; dip fillets in lemon juice mixture, and dredge in bread crumbs. Place on a baking sheet coated with cooking spray. Bake at 450 degrees F for 7 minutes; turn fillets over, and bake an additional 7 minutes or until fish flakes easily when tested with a fork. Transfer fillets to a serving platter, and top with avocado sauce.

Blackened Salmon

6 Salmon Fillets, 1/2 - 3/4 inch thick, skinned
2 1/2 cups unsalted butter or margarine
1/2 cup fresh lemon juice
1 1/2 teaspoons cayenne pepper
1 teaspoon salt
2 teaspoons fresh ground black pepper
1 Tablespoon dried thyme (do not use fresh - it will burn)
Lemon wedges and Parsley for garnish

Trim off the thin edges of fillets as these would burn. Pat dry and refrigerate until ready to cook. The butter sauce adheres better to cold fillets.

In heavy 3-quart cast-iron frying pan over medium heat, melt butter, add lemon juice, cayenne, salt, black pepper and thyme. Stir to blend; cool to lukewarm.

Place an empty 10-inch cast-iron skillet over high heat until bottom has a definite white haze and begins to smoke slightly. Remove fish from refrigerator; dip 1 fillet in warm butter sauce, coating well. Place fish in hot skillet, taking care that spits and spatters do not burn you. Fish will sear and cook almost immediately. Turn fillet over; blacken other side. Repeat with remaining fillets.

Reserve remaining butter sauce. As fillets are cooked, place them on individual plates; keep warm. Discard accumulated butter sauce in skillet and charred bits between batches. When all fillets have been cooked, wipe skillet clean and place empty skillet back on heat. Add reserved butter sauce; carefully swirl skillet 5 or 6 times to blacken butter. Remove pan from heat; drizzle butter over each fillet. Garnish and serve hot.

Bombay Monkfish

1 pound monkfish, skinned
Milk to cover
1/4 pound shrimp, shelled
2 eggs
3 tablespoons tomato paste
1/2 teaspoon curry powder
2 teaspoons lemon juice
1/4 teaspoon fresh rosemary, chopped
1 pinch of saffron or tumeric
3/4 cup light cream
Salt and pepper to taste

Preheat oven to 350F. Put the monkfish in a pan just large enough to hold it. Pour the milk over and place the pan over moderate heat. Bring to a simmer, cover, and cook for 8 minutes. Turn the fish and cook 7 minutes longer, or until the fish is cooked through. When the monkfish is nearly done, add the shrimp and cook 2-3 minutes, or until they turn pink. Drain fish and shrimp, discarding milk.

Cut the monkfish into bite-size pieces. Beat the eggs with the tomato paste, curry powder, lemon juice, rosemary, saffron and 1/2 cup cream. Mix in the fish and shrimp and season to taste with salt and pepper. Turn into 4 individual ramekin dishes and pour an equal amount of the remaining cream over the top of each dish. Bake for 20 minutes, or until set. Serve hot with a squeeze of lemon and a crusty french type bread.

Brandied Orange Rabbit With Mushrooms

4 pounds rabbit pieces
1/2 cup brandy
1/2 cup frozen orange juice concentrate
4 tablespoons butter
2 cups mushrooms, sliced
1 tablespoon cornstarch dissolved in 1/2 cup orange juice
2 cloves garlic, crushed
curry powder, to taste
salt and pepper
4 carrots, julienned

Marinate rabbit in brandy and orange juice concentrate overnight. Arrange rabbit in baking dish reserving marinade. In a skillet, melt butter and saute mushrooms until barely tender. Add reserved marinade, garlic, curry, salt and pepper. Thicken with cornstarch/orange juice mixture and pour over rabbit. Bake, uncovered, at 325F for 1 hour. Add carrots and bake 1 hour longer.

Cajun Crappie

4 Crappie fillets about 10" long
2 tablespoons butter
1 pinch cayenne pepper
3 teaspoons paprika
3 ounces cognac
1 cup heavy cream
4 tablespoons brown sugar
4 cloves crushed garlic
1 teaspoon corn starch
Ground or fresh thyme
Ground or fresh basil
Ground or fresh parsley

Combine the thyme, basil, parsley, cayenne pepper, garlic and paprika and sprinkle over fish in a shallow bowl. Melt 1 tbls. butter in a skillet and add fish, cooking until soft but not hard. Cook for 2 minutes per side. The idea is to not dry out the fish. After the fish have been cooked on both sides, remove fish and add brown sugar to pan. Then add remaining butter and return the fish to the pan once the sugar is melted. This will glaze the fish and finish cooking them. Remove fish to serving plate and deglaze skillet with cognac immediately, adding heavy cream once cognac is boiling. Reduce by 25 percent. Combine a small portion of liquid with corn starch and add to sauce.
Allow sauce to boil for about one minute. Pour sauce on top of fish and garnish with fresh parsley.

Cajun Frog Legs

16 good sized frog legs
1 cup shortening
1/2 cup flour
3 cups milk
1 teaspoon paprika
1/2 teaspoon onion powder
1/2 teaspoon garlic juice
1/2 teaspoon ground cayenne pepper
1/4 teaspoon black pepper
dash of white pepper
dash of oregano
dash of rosemary
salt to taste

Skin, clean and rinse frog legs well. Cover with whole milk and garlic juice in a plastic mixing bowl, refrigerate overnight. Pat dry, season with paprika, onion powder, cayenne, black pepper, and desired amount of salt.

Add white pepper, oregano, and rosemary to the flour. Heat shortening in a skillet. Lightly flour the frog legs and fry until golden brown.

California Wild Duck Stew

1/4 lb. fresh mushrooms, sliced
4 large tomatoes, peeled, seeded and quartered
3 tablespoons butter
1 large carrot, diced
1 medium green bell pepper, diced
1 medium onion, sliced
1 cup chopped celery and leaves
1 clove garlic, peeled and quartered
1 cup pitted ripe olives
1 tablespoon tomato paste
1/4 cup olive oil
2 cups dry red wine
1 tablespoon Worcestershire sauce
1/8 teaspoon cinnamon
1/8 teaspoon ground cloves
1/8 teaspoon allspice
1/8 teaspoon mace
1/8 teaspoon thyme
1 bay leaf, crushed
1 teaspoon salt
1/4 teaspoon freshly-ground pepper
4 wild ducks, plucked, drawn and cut into serving pieces
20 small new potatoes

Saute mushrooms and tomatoes in 3 tablespoons butter for 3 minutes. Combine with carrot, green pepper, onion, celery, garlic, olives, tomato paste, olive oil, wine, Worcestershire, cinnamon, cloves, allspice, mace, thyme, bay leaf, salt and pepper to make a marinade. Add duck pieces and marinate overnight or for at least 10 hours. Simmer duck in marinade 1 1/2 to 2 hours or until tender. Boil potatoes in salted water for approximately 15 minutes or until tender. Add to stew just before serving.

Carolina Roast Venison

5 pounds venison roast
1 onion, chopped
1/4 cup barbecue sauce, see below
1 tablespoon salt
2 tablespoon vinegar
black pepper

Barbecue Sauce:
1 tablespoon black pepper
1 tablespoon salt
1 small box dry mustard
1/4 cup sugar
1/4 cup vinegar
1/4 cup water
1 stick butter/margarine

For sauce: Mix dry ingredients. Add vinegar, water and mix. Bring to full boil and add stick of butter and continue to cook until butter melts. This makes 1 Pint of the Sauce.

Soak venison in water, vinegar and salt for 4-5 hours. Remove and wipe dry. Sprinkle lightly with pepper and brush with sauce. Add onion and enough water to cover bottom of covered roaster. Bake in 325F oven the first hour; then lower heat to 275 F for an additional 3 hours. Baste often with sauce and juices from roast.

Carp with Red Sauce

1 pound carp fillets, skinned and cut 3/8-inch thick
(cutting shortens "floating bones" so cooking can break them down)

Vegetable oil, heated in a deep fryer

Batter:
1 cup cold water
1 egg
1/4 c oil
1/4 cup flour
4 teaspoons cornstarch
1 teaspoon baking powder
1 t salt
1/2 teaspoon MSG (optional)

Mix water, egg and oil before adding other ingredients. Dip strips in batter, drop them into a deep fryer. Cook until done, drain on paper toweling. Much like hors d'oeuvres. Dip into the following sauce.

Red Sauce:
1 cup catsup
1 cup chili sauce
dash of Tabasco
dash of Worcestershire
squeeze of lemon
3 Tablespoons pure ground horseradish
salt and pepper to taste

Catfish with Parsley-Pecan Sauce

  2 cups all-purpose flour
  1 tablespoon cayenne pepper
  1 tablespoon, plus 1 teaspoon salt
  6 catfish fillets, about 6 ounces each
  2 tablespoons vegetable oil
  2 tablespoons unsalted butter
  2 cups parsley-pecan sauce

Sauce:
  2 cups tightly packed fresh parsley, leaves only
  1/2 cup olive oil
  1/2 cup broken pecan meats
  1 large clove garlic, chopped
  1/2 cup freshly grated parmesan cheese
  1/2 cup freshly grated romano cheese
  2 tablespoons unsalted butter, cut into pieces

Mix flour, cayenne pepper and salt. Spread on large platter and dredge each fillet, shaking off excess. Set aside on sheet of waxed paper. Heat half the oil and butter in a skillet large enough to accommodate 3 fillets. When butter is foaming but not brown, add fillets and saute on one side for about 4 minutes, until light golden. Turn fillets and spread the browned side with sauce; continue to saute until underside is browned, about another 4 minutes. Cover skillet for a few minutes to melt sauce. Remove fish to platter. Add remaining oil and butter and cook remaining fillets.

Sauce:

Place parsley in food processor and process until coarsely chopped, turning machine off and on and scraping down sides. Add all other ingredients except salt, and process until mixture makes a smooth paste. Store, tightly covered in refrigerator.
Makes about 2 cups.

Chinese Venison

2 lbs. venison steaks
1/4 cup soy sauce
1 cup beef bouillon
1/4 teaspoon ginger
2 cloves mashed garlic
1/4 cup sherry
4 tablespoons peanut oil
2 cloves chopped garlic
1 1/2 cups boiling water
3 large green peppers, cut into 1/2 inch strips
1 cup sliced water chestnuts
3 tablespoons cornstarch
sesame oil
hot boiled rice

Cut meat against the grain into 1/2 inch strips (this is easier to do if meat is partially frozen). Make a marinade for the meat by combining soy sauce, bouillon, ginger, mashed garlic and sherry. Marinate steak for 2-12 hours in the refrigerator. Dry meat on paper towels. In a wok, heat peanut oil and saute chopped garlic until it turns golden brown. Remove, leaving at least 2 tablespoon oil in wok. Add meat to oil and saute until brown (add just a dash of sesame oil to meat while it's browning). Add reserved marinade and 1 cup boiling water. Simmer 45 minutes or less time, if desired. When meat is tender, remove and keep in warm oven. Pour marinade in separate pan and add cornstarch. Add remaining 1/2 cup boiling water, if needed. Simmer until thick. Stir-fry green pepper and water chestnuts in liquid remaining in wok. Add meat and marinade gravy.
Add a dash of sesame oil to taste. Serve over boiled rice.

Cream Of Crab Soup

1 Small onion, finely chopped
1 Tablespoon butter
1 Cup chicken broth
1 Quart Half & Half, or whole milk
1 Tablespoon chopped parsley
1/2 Teaspoon celery salt
1/2 Teaspoon mace
1 Dash cayenne
salt and fresh ground black pepper, to taste
1 Pound crab meat, jumbo lump Maryland Blue Crab
1/4 Cup sherry
2 Tablespoons all-purpose flour,
 mixed with 1 Tablespoon water or warm milk

In a large saucepan, cook onion in butter until transparent. Add chicken broth and slowly pour in milk. Add all seasonings except sherry. Add the crab meat (cleaned of all shells) and simmer for 15 minutes.
 Make a paste of about 2 tablespoon flour and a little water or warm milk mixture. Stir paste into soup to thicken slightly. Remove from heat, stir in sherry and serve.
 Garnish with chopped parsley.

Crab Stuffing

8 ozs. Ritz crackers, crushed
1/4 lb. sweet butter, melted
1/4 cup mayonnaise
2 tablespoons chopped garlic
2 tablespoons Worcestershire sauce
1/8 cup cream sherry
1 tablspoon ground black pepper
1/2 tablespoon hot sauce
1/2 cup fresh cleaned crabmeat

In a bowl, use a small wire whisk to mix all ingredients except crackers and crab. Lightly toss in crackers and crab. This may be used to stuff shrimp or other seafood such as flounder or grouper. It's great for stuffed mushrooms, too.

Crawdad Gumbo

1 pound crawdads, cooked & cleaned
8 oz. salt pork, cubed small
1/2 pound fresh (preferred) or frozen okra
1 medium brown onion
1 can whole tomatoes
8 oz. frozen corn
1 teaspoon parsley flakes
1/2 teaspoon cayenne pepper
1 pint half & half
2 cups water
salt to taste
pepper to taste

In a large skillet, fry salt pork until browned. Add onion, cook until tender, stirring often. Add water, okra, corn, tomatoes, and all seasonings, simmer for 15-20 minutes. Add half & half, and crawdads, simmer for 10 minutes.

Deviled Rabbit

1 rabbit washed in water, then diced
4 oz. fat bacon, finely chopped
1 large onion finely chopped
8 oz. mixed carrots, leeks and turnips – diced
5 tbsp. flour
1/2 cup milk
2 cups water
1 tsp. Worcester sauce
1 tsp. curry powder
1 tsp. salt
1/2 tsp. pepper
finely chopped parsley for garnish

Saute the bacon in a large saucepan with the onion, carrots, turnips, rabbit, curry powder and Worcester sauce for 2 or 3 minutes. Add the water and bring to the boil. Season with salt and pepper and reduce the heat to low. Simmer, covered, until the rabbit is tender about 1 1/2 hours. Blend the milk and flour in a small bowl, stirring continuously, and cook until the sauce is smooth and thick. Add more salt and pepper if necessary, and serve at once, garnishing with parsley.

Duck in Guinness and Honey

1 duck, trussed
2 Tbls. oil
2 Tbls. honey
1 Tbls. brown sugar
1 cup Guinness
pinch each nutmeg and cinnamon
1 1/4 cups demiglaze or duck stock
pinch each salt and pepper

Preheat oven to 475F.
Wash and truss the duck. Brush with oil and seal in a hot oven until browned (about 10 to 12 minutes). Meanwhile, in a heavy saucepan mix together the honey, sugar, Guinness and spices and simmer for 10 minutes. Add demiglaze or stock and continue cooking for another 15 minutes.
Season to taste with salt and pepper.
Reduce heat to 300F, cover the duck with the sauce and roast for 60 to 75 minutes. Baste occasionally. Test with a fork.
If the sauce tastes too bitter at the end of cooking time, add a little more honey. Remove from the oven and allow to rest for a few minutes before carving.

Duck and Roasted Walnut Salad

2 duck breasts
Salt and freshly ground black pepper, to taste
1/2 cup walnuts

Dressing (recipe follows)

1 cucumber, halved, seeded and thinly sliced
2 tablespoons chopped green onions

Preheat oven to 350 degrees. Place duck breasts on a rack in a baking pan and season with salt and pepper; roast 45 minutes. Let cool and slice thin. Spread walnuts on a cookie sheet and roast at 350 degrees 10 to 15 minutes, or until they are brown and give off a rich, nutty aroma; stir once or twice during cooking. Prepare dressing. Toss a little dressing with cucumber slices and arrange on a platter; fan duck slices on top. Spoon reserved dressing over top and garnish with roasted walnuts and chopped onion.

Dressing:
1 tablespoon raspberry vinegar
2 tablespoons walnut oil
1 tablespoon peanut oil
1 teaspoon soy sauce
2 teaspoons sugar

In a small bowl, whisk together vinegar, oils, soy sauce and sugar. Use as directed above.

Fricassee of Rabbit

2 rabbits, about 3 pounds each, skinned and cut up
  (or similar amount of chicken)
4 egg yolks, beaten
2 cups bread crumbs
1/8 teaspoon mace
1/8 teaspoon nutmeg
1/4 cup butter for frying
2 cups brown gravy
1 cup red wine
1/2 pound fresh mushrooms, sliced
2 tablespoons each − butter and flour; mix well

Rub the rabbit pieces with the egg yolks and roll in bread crumbs to which you have added the mace and nutmeg. Fry in a dutch oven until well browned. Add the remaining ingredients and stir until thick. Cover and simmer until tender.

Fried Rocky Mountain Oysters

2 pounds bull or sheep testicles
1 cup flour
1/4 cup cornmeal
1 cup red wine
salt
black pepper
garlic powder
Louisiana Hot Sauce
pure hog lard or vegetable oil

With a very sharp knife, split the tough skin-like muscle that surrounds each "oyster." Remove the skin. Set "oysters" into a pan with enough salt water to cover them for one hour (this takes out some of the blood). Drain. Transfer "oysters" to large pot. Add enough water to float "oysters" and a generous tablespoon of vinegar. Parboil, drain and rinse. Let cool and slice each "oyster" into 1/4 inch thick ovals. Sprinkle salt and pepper on both sides of sliced "oyster" to taste.
 Mix flour, cornmeal and some garlic powder to taste in a bowl. Roll each "oyster" slice into this dry mixture. Dip into milk. Dip into dry mixture. Dip into wine quicky (you may repeat the procedure if a thicker crust is desired). Place each "oyster" into hot lard or oil. Add Louisiana Hot Sauce to lard or oil (go wild with it, buy watch out for hot splashes). Cook until golden brown or tender, and remove with a wire mesh strainer (the longer they cook, the tougher they get).

Roast Goose with Wild Rice

1 (12 pound) fresh goose
salt to taste
4 cups wild rice, cooked
2/3 cup chopped toasted hazelnuts
2 Granny Smith apples - peeled, cored and chopped
1/2 cup chopped onion
2 teaspoons ground savory
3 tablespoons chopped fresh parsley
freshly ground black pepper
1 1/2 tablespoons all-purpose flour
4 cups water

Mix together the cooked rice, nuts, apples, onion, and herbs. Season to taste with salt and pepper. Remove the neck, heart, and gizzard from the goose. Wash the bird inside and out. Pat dry. Fill the cavity of the goose with the stuffing, skewer closed, and lace string around the skewers. Truss the bird.

Roast in a preheated 325F oven, breast side down, for 1 1/2 hours. Draw off the fat as it accumulates. Turn, and roast another 1 1/2 hours. When done, the juices should run clear when the bird is pricked where the thigh attaches to the body. Remove trussing strings and skewers before carving.

While the goose is roasting, place the neck, heart, and gizzard in a saucepan with water. Let simmer gently, partially covered, for several hours, until reduced to slightly less than 2 cups. Season the broth to taste with salt.

Pour off all but 1 tablespoon of the fat from the roasting pan. Sprinkle a little flour over the bottom, 1 to 2 tablespoons, depending on how thick you like your gravy. Set the pan over low heat. Stir for 2 minutes, scraping up all the browned bits. Add the reserved goose broth to the pan, and whisk until smooth. Taste and season with salt and pepper. Serve in a gravy boat alongside the bird.

Italian Roast Pheasant

2 fresh pheasants
5 slices pancetta or bacon
1 tablespoon fresh rosemary, chopped
1 tablespoon fresh thyme, chopped
2 to 3 cloves garlic, chopped
Salt and black pepper
3/4 cup dry white wine
3 tablespoons butter
3 tablespoons brandy

Wash and dry the pheasants, removing any lumps of fat from the cavity. Make the dressing by chopping the bacon, herbs and garlic. Mix well. Spoon the dressing into the cavity and truss the birds. Season with salt and pepper.

Place the birds on their sides on a rack and bake at 350 degrees, turning every 15 minutes. The breast should remain down to keep it from drying out. After 30 minutes add the wine and continue roasting and turning the birds for another 10 to 15 minutes. Increase the heat to 450 and brown the skin. Cook the pheasant for 5 minutes on each side. Remove and keep warm.

Cut the birds in half. Place the halves, cut side down, in a large frying pan, with any stuffing that falls out and the pan juices. Add the butter, and cook over high heat for 3 to 4 minutes, or till traces of pink are gone. Add the brandy and flame them. Serve at once spooning the pan juices and stuffing on top.

Wild rice makes a fine accompaniment.

Lemon-Coriander Game Hens

2 Cornish game hens (1 1/2 pounds each), halved
1 teaspoon ground coriander
1 teaspoon ground turmeric

1/3 cup fresh lemon juice
1 green onion, minced
3 tablespoons minced fresh cilantro
2 garlic cloves, pressed

Rub game hens with coriander and turmeric. Set aside. Combine remaining ingredients in medium baking dish. Add game hens to marinade and turn to coat. Cover and refrigerate 6 hours or overnight.

Prepare barbecue (medium-high heat) or preheat broiler. Remove game hens from marinade. Season game hens with salt and pepper. Grill or broil until cooked through, turning and basting occasionally with marinade, 25 minutes.

Medieval Sweet and Sour Fish

2 pounds carp or other fish fillet
1/4 cup flour
1 medium onion, minced
3/4 cup white wine
3/4 cup cider vinegar
4 Tablespoons brown sugar
1/4 teaspoon ground cloves
1/4 cup currants
Pinch of mace
1/4 cup raisins
salt to taste

Cut fillets into large chunks and dredge them in flour. Heat oil in a large heavy frypan and saute onion until transparent. Add fish chunks and brown. In a bowl, combine remaining ingredients for a sauce. Pour over browned fish and onions.

Ostrich and Shrimp in Roasted Garlic Sauce

8 jumbo shrimp
12 pieces of ostrich, sliced medallion size and then pounded into scaloppini
15-20 medium sized whole garlic cloves, peeled
1/2 bottle of dry white wine (preferably Chardonnay)
1 1/2 pints of heavy whipping cream
1 medium sized red onion, finely chopped
1/2 stick lightly salted butter
Salt and pepper to taste
1 tbs. olive oil
1/2 cup chicken stock

Prepare ostrich and set aside. Place garlic cloves in the oven at 400F and bake until soft and brown (about 10-15 minutes). In sauce pot, melt butter and saute onion until onion is fully cooked (about 5 minutes). Add wine and allow to cook until dry over medium heat. When mixture has evaporated back down, add roasted garlic and puree. Place back on heat and slowly add cream, salt and pepper. Bring to slight boil and set aside.

In separate pan, heat olive oil add ostrich, sear on both sides and set aside. Add shrimp and chicken stock to oil; saute until cooked. Add ostrich and sauce.

Oriental Glazed Duck

1 – 5 pound duck, rinsed, patted dry
2 lemons, halved
salt and ground pepper to taste
3/4 cup soy sauce
3/4 cup ketchup
1/3 cup liquid honey
1/4 cup corn oil
4 cloves garlic, finely chopped
1 tbsp. rosemary
2 green onions, thinly sliced for garnish

Preheat oven to 400F. Rub the duck inside and out with juice of 1 lemon. Pat dry. Prick skin with fork. Sprinkle inside and outside with salt and pepper. Place second lemon in cavity. Place duck, breast side up on rack in shallow roasting pan. Bake for 30 minutes. While duck is roasting, make glaze. Combine soy sauce, ketchup, honey, oil, garlic and rosemary in small mixing bowl. Mix well. Reduce oven temperature to 350F. Pour off fat. Pour glaze over duck. Baste frequently and cook 1 hour and 15 minutes. Remove duck from oven. Let stand 15 minutes. Skim off fat from roasting pan. Reheat glaze, pour over duck and garnish with green onions.

Chunky Oyster Chowder

1 pint oysters
1/4 cup melted butter
1/2 cup sauteed sliced celery
1 quart milk
1 1/2 teaspoons salt
1/8 teaspoon pepper
1/2 teaspoon paprika
1/2 cup sauteed chopped Onion
1 can undrained whole kernel corn
1 cup cooked diced potatoes

Open and save, or drain and save the oysters reserving the liquor. Remove any remaining shell particles. Add oysters and liquor to butter and cook for 3 minutes or until edges of oysters begin to curl. Add milk, onion, celery, corn, potatoes, salt & pepper; heat thoroughly but do not boil. Garnish with paprika. Serve at once.

Panfish Creole

1 1/2 lbs. panfish (sunfish, bluegill, perch)
1/4 cup flour
1/3 cup cooking oil
1 1/4 cup hot water
1 - 8 oz. can tomato sauce
1/2 cup chopped green onions and tops
1/2 cup chopped parsley
1/3 cup chopped green peppers
5 small cloves garlic chopped fine
2 teaspoons salt
1/2 tespoon thyme
1/4 teaspoon cayenne pepper
2 whole bay leaves
1 lemon slice
2 1/2 cups cooked rice

Cut fish in one inch chunks. Coat fish in flour and brown in oil stirring constantly. Add water gradually. Cook until smooth and thisk stirring constantly. Add remaining ingredients except rice. Cover and simmer for 20 minutes. Remove bay leaves and serve over rice.

Partridge Casserole

6 partridge
12 slices of bacon
6 slices of cooked ham
1/2 cup brandy
1/2 cup butter
3/4 cup beef stock
2 1/4 cup orange juice
Salt and pepper, to taste

Preheat oven to 400F.
Clean, wash, stuff, and truss partridge. Cover breasts with bacon slices. Line casserole with ham slices. Arrange birds in casserole, then cover.
Cook over low heat for 15 minutes. Remove cover to pour brandy over birds. Cover again and bake for 20 minutes at 400F. Remove birds and ham. Skim off fat, then strain pan juices.
Gradually add butter and beef stock to juices, stirring constantly while bringing them to a boil. Add orange juice, salt, and pepper. Return birds and ham to sauce, then serve.

Pheasant Jubilee

4 pheasants, quartered
Flour
1/2 butter or maragarine
1 onion chopped
1/2 cup golden raisins
1 cup chili sauce
1/2 water
1/2 brown sugar
2 tablespoons Worchesershire sauce
1/4 teaspoon garlic powder
1 cup Sherry
1 (1-lb.) can pitted dark sweet cherries, drained

Dust pheasants with flour. Melt butter in a heavy skillet: brown birds thoroughly. Place pheasants in a deep casserole. In the same skillet, combine onion, raisins, chili sauce, water, brown sugar, Worchesterhire sauce and garlic; boil briefly, scraping browned meat from bottom and sides of pan; pour over pheasants. Bake covered, in a moderately slow oven (325F) for 1 1/2 hours. remove cover; add sherry and cherries. Continue baking 20 minutes longer. To serve, transfer to a deep chafing or warming dish. This works well with wild rice and a fresh green vegetable.

Pheasant in Spiced Sour Cream

1 Pheasant – Cut up
Flour
Butter
8 oz. Sour Cream
2 Cups Water
2 teaspoons Worcestershire Sauce
Few drops Tabasco Sauce
2 Bay Leaves
Dash Sweet Basil
Dash Rosemary
Salt and Pepper

Dust pieces of pheasant with flour and brown in butter. Mix sour cream and water. Add remaining ingredients to sour cream mixture. Pour sour cream mixture in a covered roaster and add pheasant. Bake at 325F for several hours or until tender.

Rabbit In Tarragon Sauce

2 rabbits, cut into serving pieces
Salt and pepper
4 tablespoons olive oil
1 cup onion, chopped
1 cup carrot, peeled and chopped
1 cup celery, chopped
Flour
2 cans chicken broth
1/2 cup sherry
2 teaspoons tarragon
1 cup heavy whipping cream
1 tablespoon Dijon mustard
1/4 cup parsley, minced

Season rabbit with salt and pepper. Place olive oil in skillet and brown rabbit. Remove meat and drain on paper towel. Add onion, carrot and celery to skillet. Saute 5 minutes. Stir in enough flour to make a paste. Blend in broth, sherry and tarragon. Return rabbit to skillet. Bring sauce to a boil and reduce heat to simmer. Baste meat frequently for 45-60 minutes. Remove rabbit to serving platter and keep warm in oven. Strain and degrease sauce, discarding vegetables. Return remaining sauce to skillet and add cream. Simmer until thickened, stirring frequently. Remove from heat and add mustard and parsley. Pour sauce over rabbit and serve.

Rack of Venison With Mushrooms

1 quart beef stock
1/2 cup chopped leeks
1/4 cup each, chopped: shallots and carrot
1 tomato, chopped
1/2 bunch fresh parsley (leaves only)
1/2 cup port wine
2 teaspoons tomato paste
1 rack of venison (8 ribs, about 2 pounds)
1/4 cup olive oil
2 cups sliced mixed exotic mushrooms (oyster, shiitake, portobello)
Salt and freshly ground black pepper, to taste
Chopped parsley or watercress for garnish (optional)

In a very large saucepan, combine stock, leeks, shallots, carrot, tomato and parsley; whisk in port and tomato paste. Bring to a slow boil, reduce heat and simmer 2 hours, or until sauce is reduced to 3 cups. Strain and discard solids. Preheat oven to 425F.

Place venison on a rack in a roasting pan and roast 25 minutes, just to medium rare. Remove venison from oven and set aside. (To add an optional crust on the top, brush 1 tablespoon Dijon mustard over roasted venison. Pat on about 1/2 to 3/4 cup dry seasoned bread crumbs. Return venison to oven until bread crumbs are browned.)

Meanwhile, heat oil in skillet and add mushrooms; saute briefly, then season with salt and pepper. Pour about 1/4 cup sauce on each of 8 plates. Place 2 slices venison on each plate, atop sauce. Garnish with mushrooms and chopped parsley.

Roast Duck with Port-Garlic Sauce

For sauce:
 1 5-pound duck, fresh or frozen, thawed (neck, heart and gizzard reserved)
 1 medium onion, quartered
 1 carrot, coarsely chopped
 1 celery stalk, coarsely chopped
 4 1/2 cups water

 2 tablespoons (1/4 stick) butter
 6 large garlic cloves, sliced
 1 cup ruby Port
 1 tablespoon all purpose flour

For duck:
 1/3 cup soy sauce
 3 tablespoons Dijon mustard
 3 large garlic cloves, pressed
 1 teaspoon coarse salt
 1 teaspoon ground pepper
 1 teaspoon dried thyme

Cut off duck wing tips at joint. Combine neck, heart, gizzard and wing tips in large saucepan. Add onion, carrot and celery to pan. Add 4 1/2 cups water and bring to boil. Reduce heat and simmer 1 hour. Strain stock into medium saucepan. Boil stock until reduced to 1 cup, about 15 minutes.

Melt 1 tablespoon butter in heavy large skillet over medium heat. Add sliced garlic and saute until golden, about 2 minutes. Add Port and boil 5 minutes. Add reduced duck stock and boil until reduced to 1 cup, about 8 minutes. Mix remaining 1 tablespoon butter and flour in small bowl. Whisk into sauce and simmer until thickened, about 1 minute. Season sauce with salt and pepper.

Preheat oven to 400F. Trim excess fat from cavity of duck. Using fork, pierce duck skin in several places. Place duck, breast side up, on rack in large roasting pan. Brush soy sauce over duck. Mix mustard and pressed garlic in small bowl. Brush mustard mixture over duck. Mix salt, pepper and thyme in another small bowl. Sprinkle spice-herb mixture over duck and in cavity. Roast duck 45 minutes. Turn duck and roast, breast side down, 30 minutes.

Turn duck and roast, breast side up, until duck is deep golden brown and cooked through, about 15 minutes longer.

Transfer duck to platter. Serve with warmed sauce.

Roast Goose with Baked Apples

6 – 8 firm medium apples, cored
1 cup mashed cooked sweet potatoes
1/4 cup packed brown sugar
2 tablespoons melted butter
1/4 teaspoon salt
Dash of pepper
1 whole wild goose, 6-8 pounds
Seasoned salt
Salt and pepper
1 carrot, cut into 1-inch pieces
1 stalk celery, cut into 1-inch pieces
1 medium onion, cut into 8 pieces
Apple brandy

Remove a thin strip of peel from the top of each apple. In medium mixing bowl, combine remaining apple ingredients and mix well.
Stuff apples with sweet potato mixture, mounding on top. Place in shallow baking dish. Set apples aside. Heat oven to 325F.
Pat goose dry with paper towels. Sprinkle cavity lightly with seasoned salt, salt, and pepper. Place carrot, celery, and onion in cavity.
Tie drumsticks across cavity. Tuck wing tips behind back. Place, breast side up, on rack in roasting pan. Sprinkle outside of goose with seasoned salt, salt, and pepper.
Roast, basting frequently with pan juices and sprinkling occasionally with brandy, until desired doneness, about 20-25 minutes per pound. Drain and discard excess fat during roasting.
Place stuffed apples in oven during last 30-45 minutes of roasting. Baste apples frequently with goose drippings.
Remove apples when fork-tender. Allow goose to rest 20 minutes before carving and serving.

Roast Quail Stuffed with Foie Gras

4 quail, boned
Salt and pepper
Pate de foie gras (enough to stuff quail, about 2 ounces each)
4 pieces of bacon
3 tablespoons unsalted butter
1/3 cup minced shallot
1/4 cup Armagnac
1 1/2 cups veal or chicken stock
2 to 3 teaspoons arrowroot dissolved in water
Fresh chervil for garnish

Preheat oven to 350F. Season quail, stuff with foie gras and wrap with bacon. In oven proof saute pan heat 2 tablespoons of the butter over moderate heat until hot. Add quail and cook until golden on all sides. Transfer to oven and roast 15 minutes. Transfer quail to a serving dish.

Discard all but 2 tablespoons fat from pan. Add shallot and cook, stirring, 1 minute. Deglaze pan with Armagnac, scraping up brown bits clinging to bottom of pan. Add veal stock and reduce to 1 cup. Add enough arrowroot to lightly thicken sauce. Whisk in remaining butter. Pour juices from platter containing quail into sauce and stir to combine. Coat quail with sauce and garnish with chervil.

Roast Wild Turkey

1 wild turkey 8 to 10 lbs
1 lb. of pork sausage
1/2 cup of butter
1/2 lb. of sliced mushrooms
2 stalks of chopped celery
1 chopped onion
2 garlic cloves, minced
6 cups of bread cubes
1 egg

Preheat oven to 325F.

If the wild taste is something you do not like, marinate the turkey in buttermilk for 24 hours.

Brown the pork sausage in a skillet and drain the grease. Add the butter, mushroom, garlic, onion, and celery to skillet and melt the butter. Pour the mix over the bread cubes in a bowl and stir in the egg. Clean inside and out and dry the turkey.

Stuff the prepared dressing into the cavity and place turkey in a roasting pan. Place a meat thermometer in the breast of the turkey avoiding the bones. Lightly rub oil over the turkey.

Cover the turkey loosely with foil. Place roasting pan in oven for about 3 1/2 hours, occasionally basting with oil or butter. Remove the foil and continue to roast for 30 min. The turkey is done when the thermometer reads 185F.

Pull the turkey from the oven and let sit for 30 min.

Salmon Pate

1 cup salmon, flaked
1 pkg. (8 oz.) cream cheese, room temperature
1 tablespoon fresh lemon juice
1 teaspoon prepared horseradish
1 teaspoon onion, grated
1/4 teaspoon salt
1/8 teaspoon pepper
1/8 teaspoon liquid smoke

Garnish:
almond slices
parsley
1 olive
celery

Mix salmon with all of the other ingredients. Press into a fish shaped mold or shape by hand as such. Garnish fish with almond slices to resemble scales. Slice green olive for eye and thin strips of celery for tail. Garnish top with parsley. Chill at least 1 hour before serving.

Scotched Pheasant

1 pheasant
1 tablespoon Grey Poupon or other not-bright-yellow mustard
1/4 cup olive oil
1 tablespoon rosemary
1/4 cup scotch (wine will do if you don't have scotch)
1/4 cup chicken broth

Fillet the pheasant breast and cut off the legs (skinned).
Cover all four pieces in the mustard and brown them in olive oil in a pan. Sprinkle the meat with the rosemary and add the scotch and the chicken broth.
Bring the liquid to a boil, then lower the heat and cover. Simmer for 7 to 8 minutes, then uncover. The breast pieces should be done. Remove them and let the legs cook until the sauce thickens.

Baked Seafood Au Gratin

1 onion, chopped
1 green bell pepper, chopped
1 cup butter
1 cup all-purpose flour
1 pound fresh crab meat
4 cups water
1 pound medium shrimp, peeled and deveined
1/2 pound bay scallops
1/2 pound flounder fillets
3 cups milk
1 cup shredded sharp Cheddar cheese
1 tablespoon distilled white vinegar
1 teaspoon Worcestershire sauce
1/2 teaspoon salt
1 pinch ground black pepper
dash hot red pepper sauce
1/2 cup grated Parmesan cheese

Lightly grease one 13x9x2 inch baking dish. In a heavy skillet, saute the onion and the pepper in 1/2 cup of the butter or margarine. Cook until tender. Stir in 1/2 cup of the flour and cook over medium heat for 10 minutes, stirring frequently. Add the crabmeat and stir well. Press this mixture into the bottom of the prepared baking dish and set aside.

In a large Dutch oven, bring the water to a boil. Add the shrimp, scallops and flounder. Simmer for 3 minutes. Drain and reserve 1 cup of the cooking liquid and set the seafood aside.

Preheat oven to 350F. In a heavy saucepan, melt the remaining 1/2 cup butter over low heat. Stir in the remaining 1/2 cup flour. Cook and stir constantly for 1 minute. Gradually add the milk plus the 1 cup reserved cooking liquid. Raise heat to medium and cook, stirring constantly, until the mixture is thickened and bubbly. Stir in the shredded Cheddar cheese, vinegar, Worcestershire sauce, salt, pepper, and hot sauce. Add the cooked seafood and stir gently.

Spoon the seafood mixture over the crabmeat crust and sprinkle with the Parmesan cheese. Bake in the preheated oven for 30 minutes or until lightly browned. Serve immediately.

Spicy Blackened Catfish

2 teaspoons sweet paprika
1/2 teaspoon dried oregano, crumbled
1/2 teaspoon dried thyme, crumbled
1/4 teaspoon cayenne, or to taste
1/2 teaspoon sugar
1/2 teaspoon salt
1/4 teaspoon freshly ground black pepper
2 catfish fillets (about 1 pound)
1 large garlic clove, sliced thin
1 tablespoon olive oil
1 tablespoon unsalted butter
lemon wedges as an accompaniment

In a small bowl combine the paprika, oregano, thyme, cayenne, sugar, salt, and black pepper. Pat the catfish dry, and sprinkle the spice mixture on both sides of the fillet, coating them well. In a large skillet saute the garlic in the oil over moderately high heat, stirring, until it is golden brown and discard the garlic. Add the butter, heat it until the foam subsides, and in the fat, saute the catfish for 4 minutes on each side, or until it is cooked through. Transfer the catfish fillets with a slotted spatula to 2 plates and serve them with the lemon wedges.

Tarragon Trout

   2 trout with heads on (8-10 oz.)
   1/4 cup water
   1/4 cup olive oil
   1/2 tablespoon tarragon leaves
   1/2 cup white vinegar
   1 tablespoon Dijon mustard
   1/2 tablespoon minced shallots
   1/4 teaspoon salt
   1/4 teaspoon black pepper

Combine tarragon leaves and vinegar in a saucepan and bring to a boil. Cool, and add the remaining ingredients. Pour the marinade over the trout. Refrigerate for 3-4 hours. Cook the trout on a charcoal grill for 3 to 4 minutes brushing occasionally with marinade.

Trout with Red Onion and Orange Relish

1 - 1 1/3-pound trout, boned, cut in half lengthwise
yellow cornmeal
salt and pepper to taste
1 medium orange
3 tablespoons chopped fresh mint
2 tablespoons olive oil
2/3 cup chopped red onion
2 tablespoons white wine vinegar

Grate 1 teaspoon peel from orange. Cut off remaining peel and discard. Cut orange into 1/2-inch pieces. Mix orange pieces, peel and mint in small bowl. Heat 1/2 tablespoon oil in heavy large skillet over medium heat. Add onion, then vinegar. Toss until just heated through, about 1 minute. Add onion mixture to orange mixture (do not clean skillet). Season relish with salt and pepper.
Sprinkle fish with salt and pepper. Sprinkle on all sides with cornmeal. Heat remaining 1 1/2 tablespoons oil in same skillet over medium-high heat. Add fish and saute until crisp outside and just opaque in center, about 4 minutes per side. Transfer fish to plates; top with relish.

Venison Bigos

1/2 pound venison, cubed
1/2 pound lean pork, cubed
1/2 pound venison sausage, sliced 1/2" thick
1/2 pound bacon, diced
1 can beef broth, (10 1/2 oz)
1 large onion, diced
8 ounces fresh mushrooms, sliced
1 cup red wine
1 tablespoon mild paprika
salt and pepper, to taste
2 cans sauerkraut, (32 oz total)

In a Dutch oven, fry the bacon until crisp, then remove and drain, leaving grease in pan. Saute onion and mushrooms in drippings until softened, then remove and drain them. Pour off all but 1/4 cup of drippings. Brown the meats. Add the bacon, onions, mushrooms, and remaining ingredients, except sauerkraut. Bring to a simmer, stirring. Cover and simmer for 2 hours. Add drained sauerkraut and simmer 20 more minutes.

Venison Cutlets with Apples

1 slice venison, 1/2 inch thick
4 apples
Powdered sugar
1/3 cup port wine
Salt and pepper to taste
Butter
12 candied cherries

Wipe, core, and cut apples in 1/4-inch size slices. Sprinkle with powdered sugar; add wine, cover, and let stand 30 minutes. Drain (reserving wine) and saute in butter. Cut venison in cutlets, sprinkle with salt and pepper, and cook 3 to 4 minutes in lightly greased pan. Remove from pan. Melt 3 tablespoons butter in pan; add wine drained from apples and cherries. Reheat cutlets in sauce and serve with apples.

Venison Sirloin

3 pieces of 2 oz. venison medallions
1 oz. clarified butter or oil
1 tbsp. chopped shallots
1 teas. chopped parsley
1 teas. chopped thyme
1 teas. chopped tarragon
4 oz. sliced wild mushrooms
2 tbsp. grained mustard
4 oz. heavy cream
2 oz. cognac
flour for dusting
salt & pepper to taste

In hot pan add butter. Dredge medallions in flour. Saute quickly. Take out of pan and add shallots and herbs. Saute. Add mushrooms and flambe with cognac. Add heavy cream and reduce until desired thickness. Wisk in mustard. Add seasonings and medallions. Serve.

Venison Stew

Spice Mix:
  2 tablespoons paprika
  3/4 teaspoon thyme
  1/2 teaspoon curry powder
  1/2 teaspoon ground cumin
  3/4 teaspoon cayenne pepper
  3/4 teaspoon dry mustard
  1/2 teaspoon black pepper

Stew:
  5 pounds venison (chuck or leg meat), cut into 1-inch cubes
  1/2 cup vegetable oil, divided
  3/4 pound dried apricots
  1/2 pound dried prunes
  1 cup dry red wine
  6 cups beef broth
  3 cups chicken broth
  3/4 cup butter
  3/4 cup flour
  3/4 pound onions, chopped
  1/2 cup chopped parsley
  Salt and pepper to taste

  Stir together ingredients for Spice Mix and set aside. In a large bowl, place venison and toss with entire spice mixture. Cover with plastic wrap, set in the refrigerator and leave overnight.
  On cooking day, combine dried fruit and red wine in bowl, and set aside. Heat a large saute pan until very hot, add a little oil. Add meat in batches and replenish oil as needed to brown meat well on all sides. Remove meat to 8-quart stock pot as it browns. Deglaze saute pan with a bit of stock to melt drippings. Transfer drippings to stock pot along with the rest of beef and chicken stock.
  Bring to a boil, reduce heat to simmer, cover and cook 2 hours or until meat is tender. When meat is done, strain off and save the cooking liquid. Set meat aside temporarily.
  In same stock pot, which you have now emptied, melt butter and cook until it bubbles, but doesn't burn. Stir or whisk in flour. Brown it lightly to make a roux. Slowly add strained-off cooking liquid to make a sauce. Add enough liquid for desired thickness. Let simmer 5 minutes. Add meat, dried fruit and wine. Meanwhile, saute onions

in a small amount of oil. Add to stew with parsley, salt and pepper to taste.

Venison Roast Marinated in Buttermilk

    4-5 pound venison leg roast

Rub the roast well with a mixture of:
  1 tablespoon coarse ground black pepper
  2 teaspoons ground red chile pepper
  1 teaspoon thyme
  1 teaspoon sage
  1 tablespoon vinegar.

Let roast sit a couple hours, then marinate in:
  4 sliced onions
  4-5 bay leaves
  6 cloves garlic, crushed
  1 teaspoon whole black peppercorns
  Small stick of cinnamon
  1/2 gallon buttermilk

Place in refrigerater for 2-3 days, turning occasionally.

Drain roast, discard marinade. Brown roast well in a bit of bacon grease in a dutch oven. Drain grease. Add a bottle of good beer or cider. Cover and bake slowly, 300-325F for an hour or two. Add a couple onions, carrots, a couple apples and a sweet potato or two. Add more beer, cider or water to maintain liquid level. Continue to roast until vegetables and roast are tender.
Serve with a green salad and corn bread.

Wild Goose Chase

1 cup dried apricots, halved
2 cups dried prunes, halved
1/2 cup Madeira wine
1 goose (12 pounds)
juice of 1 orange
2 tart apples
grated zest of 1 orange
salt and pepper to taste
dash paprika
8 slices bacon
1 1/4 cups Wild Goose Sauce (recipe below)

Place apricots and prunes in mixing bowl. Add Madeira. Mix and set aside.

Preheat oven to 325F. Rinse goose and pat dry. Prick all over with fork. Rub inside and out with orange juice. Add apples and orange zest to apricots and prunes. Sprinkle goose inside and out with salt, pepper and paprika. Stuff cavity with fruit. Skewer opening closed. Lay bacon slices across breast. Place goose, breast side up, in shallow roasting pan. Roast for 1 1/2 hours, removing accumulated fat every 30 minutes. Remove bacon and roast for 1 hour more, removing fat after 30 minutes. Remove from oven. Let stand 20 minutes before carving.

Make sauce:
  pan drippings from roasted goose
  2 green onions, chopped
  3/4 cup chicken stock
  1/2 cup Madeira wine
  1 tbsp. peppercorns, slightly crushed
  1 tsp. cornstarch
  salt and fresh ground pepper to taste

Scrape brown pan drippings into saucepan. Add green onions, 1/2 cup stock, Madeira and peppercorns. Simmer 5 minutes. Mix cornstarch with remaining 1/4 cup stock until smooth. Slowly drizzle into sauce, stirring rapidly. Add salt and pepper. Stir, simmer 5 minutes. Serve over goose.

www.ingramcontent.com/pod-product-compliance
Lightning Source LLC
LaVergne TN
LVHW081545060526
838200LV00048B/2224